# Graphing

by Jennifer Boothroyd

first step nonfiction

Lerner Publications Company · Minneapolis

We like different colors.

Let's make a graph.

Five of us like green.

Three of us like red.

Two of us like yellow.

Six of us like blue.

How many like orange?